GORDON PARKS

How the Photographer Captured
Black and White America

Carole Boston Weatherford

illustrations by
Jamey Christoph

Albert Whitman & Company
Chicago, Illinois

*T*he youngest of fifteen, Parks arrives stillborn
and is nearly left for dead until a dip
in ice water shocks his tiny heart to beat.

The baby is named for the man who saved his life,
Dr. Gordon.

When young Gordon crosses the prairie on horseback, nothing seems beyond reach.

But his white teacher tells her all-black class,
You'll all wind up porters and waiters.

What did she know?

After Gordon loses
his mother at age fourteen,
he moves in with his sister
in Minneapolis.

Soon on his own,
Gordon works odd jobs:
busboy, piano player,
and finally
porter and waiter.

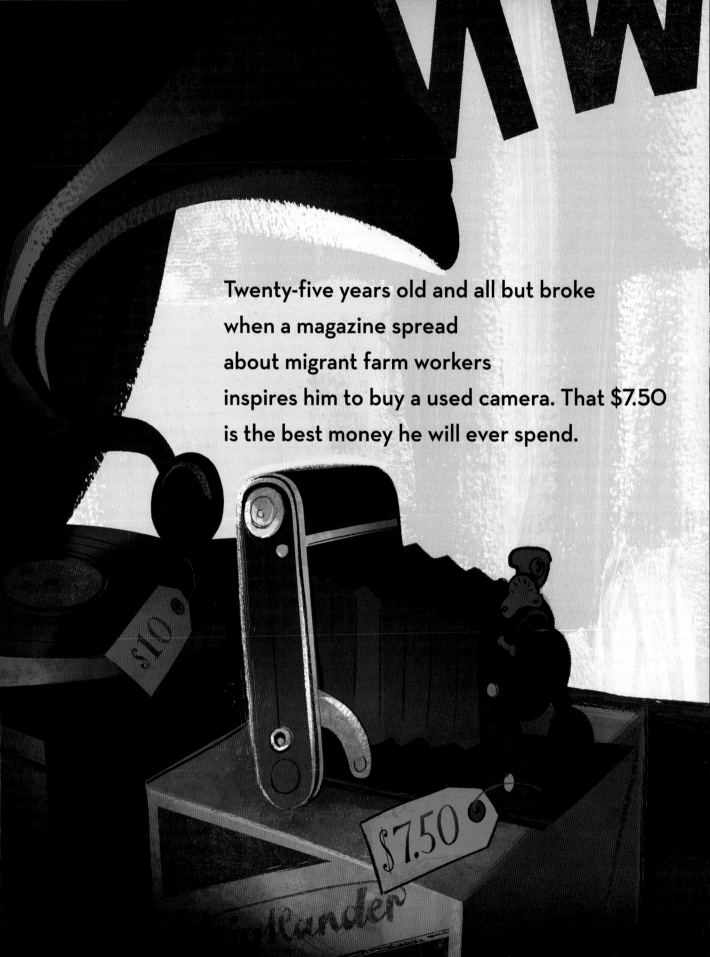

Twenty-five years old and all but broke
when a magazine spread
about migrant farm workers
inspires him to buy a used camera. That $7.50
is the best money he will ever spend.

In one month he teaches himself enough
for an exhibit at a camera store.

Soon, he is shooting fashion and portraits.
One model tells him to take
his camera to the big city.

In Chicago, Gordon's shots
of struggling families
on the South Side
win him a chance to be
a government photographer.

He leaves the Midwest
and turns his camera
on Washington.

In the nation's capital, he passes
the White House
and the Supreme Court.

In the shadow of the Capitol,
he sees black families living in alley dwellings.
He can see that blacks have it harder than whites.

He passes statues, monuments,
and memorials to mighty heroes.

But there are enough photos
of white men carved
in marble and granite.

He glimpses whites-only signs
in shop windows and learns firsthand
that even if there is no sign,
it doesn't mean that a black man
will be served.

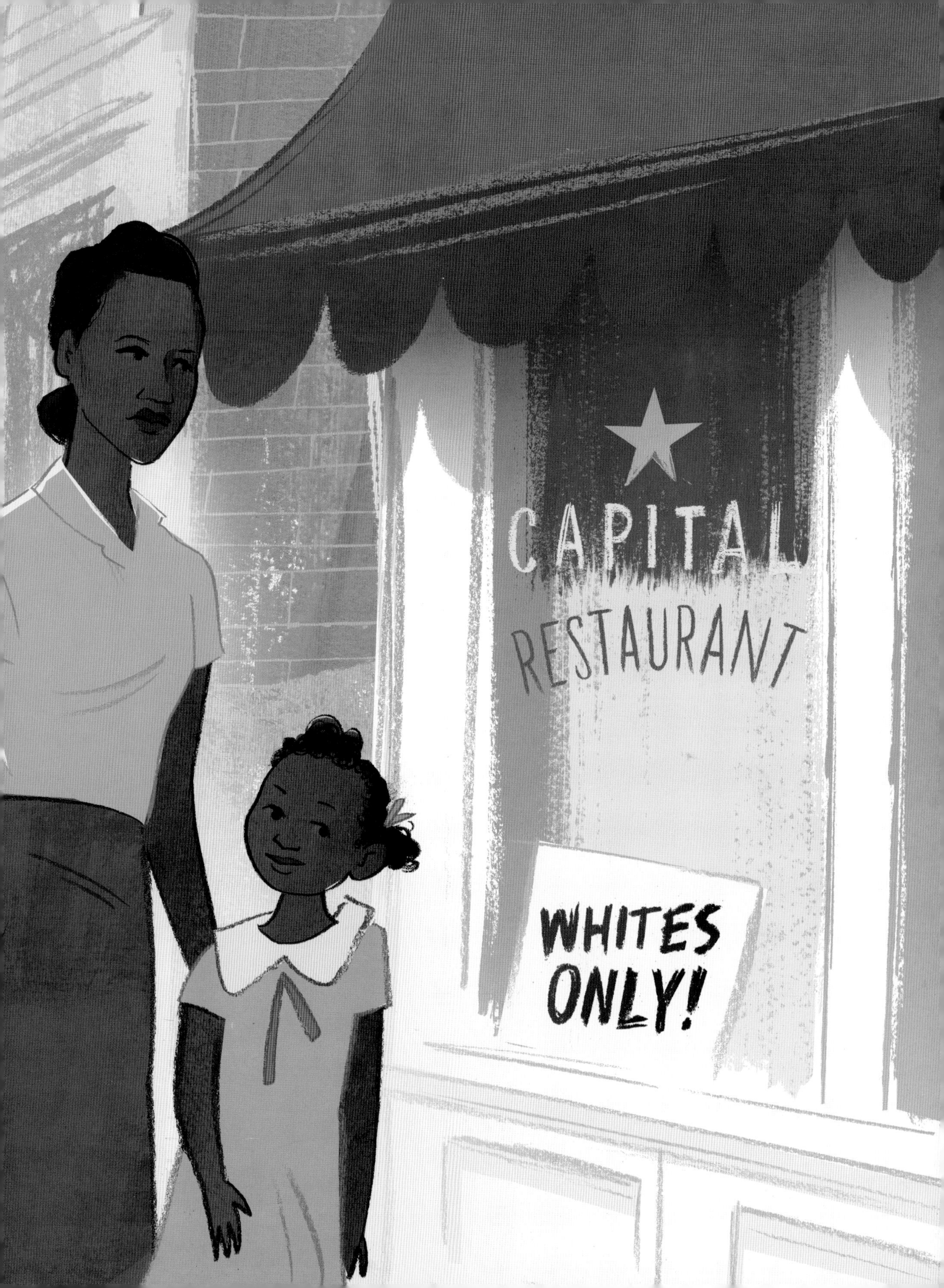
CAPITAL
RESTAURANT
WHITES ONLY!

Boiling mad, Parks vows to lay bare racism
with his lens. He shares his vision
with his boss, who points him toward his subject.

Talk to her.
She knows struggle.

She is Ella Watson, a cleaning lady in the building where Parks works. She supports five children on just over one thousand dollars a year.

The photographer
follows her for weeks.

Home.

Church.

And to work
at four in the morning.

After a long day, she studies
the Bible with her family.

Gordon takes pictures
of her grandchildren too.

Dressing.

Eating.

Reading.

Playing.

Not yet knowing the racism
that they will surely face.

Over his long career,
Gordon's photos will run
in *Vogue* and *Life* magazines—
their first black photographer.

He will write novels, make movies,
compose music and poetry,
and be hailed a Renaissance man.

LIFE

VOGUE

GORDON PARKS

Tree Symphony
by
Gordon Parks

But Gordon's most famous shot will be American Gothic.

In the newspaper, the photo
exposed to the nation
the unfairness of segregation.

Standing before
the flag of freedom,
cleaning lady Ella Watson
holds the tools of her trade
and the hopes of
her grandchildren.

She knows all too well
that the opportunities
the flag symbolizes are denied her
because of skin color.

Yet, she dares to dream of—and strive for—better.

Through Gordon's lens,
her struggle gained a voice.

You don't have to hear her story
to know her prayer.

ABOUT GORDON PARKS

Gordon Parks was one of the most important photographers of the 20th century. Through art—photography, music, literature, and film—he pursued what he called "the common search for a better life and a better world."

Born on November 30, 1912, in Fort Scott, Kansas, Parks was the youngest of fifteen children. His father, Andrew, was a tenant farmer and his mother, Sarah, died when he was fifteen. He then moved to St. Paul, Minnesota, where he lived with his sister for a short time and attended high school until he was forced to quit. He held various odd jobs, including that of singer and piano player. While working as a railroad porter, he was so moved by a magazine photo spread about migrant workers that he bought a camera at a pawnshop.

Although self-taught, he soon became a portrait and fashion photographer and landed an exhibition at an Eastman Kodak store. Marva Louis, a model and the wife of boxing champion Joe Louis, suggested that Parks move to a big city to further his career. He chose Chicago. A photo-essay that Parks shot on Chicago's South Side won him a fellowship to photograph social conditions in America for the Farm Security Administration, a government agency based in Washington DC.

During his first days with the Farm Security Administration (FSA), Parks—stunned by racial segregation in the capital—shot his defining photograph of cleaning woman Ella Watson. Mrs. Watson supported two grandchildren and an adopted daughter on a salary of less than $1,000 a year. The iconic photograph of her holding a broom and a mop against a backdrop of the American flag would become known as "American Gothic." In one iconic photo, Parks conveyed both the African American struggle against racism and the contradiction between segregation and freedom.

After the FSA closed in 1943, Parks built a successful career as a photographer for leading magazines such as *Life* and *Vogue*. As *Life's* first black staff photographer and writer, Parks photographed racism and poverty, as well as leaders and celebrities. Committed to social justice, he not only documented but also served as an advocate for the Civil Rights Movement.

In his later years, Parks proved to be a Renaissance man. He stretched artistically by experimenting with color photography, writing novels and poetry, composing music, and writing and directing films. In 1963 he published the coming-of-age novel *The Learning Tree*. In 1969, when the book became a movie, Parks was the first African American to write and direct a feature film. He also directed the 1971 hit movie *Shaft*.

A humanitarian as well as an artist, Parks was awarded the National Medal of Arts in 1988 and held more than fifty honorary doctorate degrees. He died in 2006.

Government charwoman ("American Gothic"), 1942

Government charwoman cleaning after regular working hours, 1942

A dance group, 1942

A sample of Gordon Parks's photos for the Farm Security Administration featuring his captions

Harlem newsboy, 1943

AUTHOR'S NOTE

I grew up seeing Gordon Parks's photos on the pages of *Life* magazine. I once met Parks at a Morgan State University exhibition of his experimental color photographs. Years later, I discovered his Farm Security Administration photographs while researching pictures for my poetry collection *Remember the Bridge*. It was then that my Aunt Helen told me she had worked with Parks during his stint in Washington. And, they had been friends. After Aunt Helen's death, her best friend gave me a photo of my aunt outdoors in Washington in the early 1940s. I sense Parks's hand and vision in that shot. But I will never know if he was behind the lens.

Library of Congress Cataloging-in-Publication data is on file with the publisher.

Text copyright © 2015 by Carole Boston Weatherford
Illustrations copyright © 2015 by Jamey Christoph
Photographs by Gordon Parks, photographer, Library of Congress, Prints & Photographs Division,
LC-DIG-fsa-8b14845, LC-DIG-ppmsca-05811, LC-DIG-fsa-8b37532, LC-DIG-fsa-8d28520
Published in 2015 by Albert Whitman & Company
ISBN 978-0-8075-3017-7

Printed in China.
10 9 8 7 6 5 4 3 2 1 HH 20 19 18 17 16 15 14
Designed by Jordan Kost

For more information about Albert Whitman & Company,
visit our web site at www.albertwhitman.com.